CW01149866

Original title:
Starting Over

Copyright © 2024 Swan Charm
All rights reserved.

Author: Sara Säde
ISBN HARDBACK: 978-9916-89-994-6
ISBN PAPERBACK: 978-9916-89-995-3
ISBN EBOOK: 978-9916-89-996-0

The Rhythm of Renewal

In the dawn's gentle light, we awake,
Soft whispers of nature, a world to remake.
Leaves dance in the breeze, a vibrant embrace,
Each moment's a gift, a chance to find space.

With each heartbeat, the earth starts to stir,
New blooms arise, their colors a blur.
The song of the river flows endlessly on,
A melody sweet, as day greets the dawn.

As shadows retreat, the sun warms the ground,
Encouraging life in the silence profound.
We gather our dreams like seeds in a hand,
Planting our futures in this fertile land.

Time weaves a tapestry rich and diverse,
We learn through our trials, embrace the reverse.
In the heartbeat of change, there's beauty so rare,
A rhythm of cycles that teaches us care.

So let us rejoice in each season's own tale,
For in every ending, new beginnings unveil.
With gratitude, we stand, through the joy and the pain,
In the rhythm of life, we find hope again.

Mosaic of New Paths

Woven threads of bright delight,
Footsteps on a road of light.
Every choice a vibrant hue,
Painting dreams in skies so blue.

Shadows whisper tales untold,
Guiding hearts both brave and bold.
Each detour a chance to learn,
In the fire of life we burn.

The Symphony of Change

With every note, the world will shift,
Melodies, both tender and swift.
In the chorus of the brave,
New horizons we all crave.

Rhythms dance through time and space,
Transforming each and every face.
In this song of human grace,
We embrace the bright embrace.

Redefining the Journey

Maps are drawn in fading ink,
Paths obscure, we pause and think.
Step by step, we navigate,
Finding love at every gate.

Every stumble, every fall,
Teaches us to stand up tall.
In the maze, we find our way,
Crafting dreams in light of day.

The Canvas of Hope

Strokes of color on the page,
Whispers fuel the heart's engage.
With each brush, the scene unfolds,
In bright hues, our tale is told.

Layers deep, emotions blend,
Creating visions without end.
In this masterpiece, we cope,
Painting futures filled with hope.

Navigating New Skies

In the dawn's light we sail,
Charting dreams on a trail.
Winds whispering tales of flight,
Hearts ignited with pure delight.

Clouds dance in a vibrant swirl,
The vast unknown begins to unfurl.
Stars guide us through the night,
In every shadow, there's hope and light.

Each wave a story to tell,
Of courage we know so well.
With every turn, we grow strong,
In this journey, we belong.

Hands raised to touch the sun,
A new adventure has begun.
With the horizon calling clear,
We embrace the world without fear.

Together we'll navigate time,
In harmony, our spirits climb.
The sky above, our endless sea,
Navigating new skies, wild and free.

The Bridge to Tomorrow

A path stretches wide and vast,
Linking dreams both pure and fast.
With each step, hope takes flight,
Beneath the stars, we find our light.

Hands clasped in unity's grace,
Together we'll explore this space.
Through the fog, our vision shines,
In the morning, our future aligns.

We rise to greet the dawn,
Fears laid down, we carry on.
The bridge can hold our whispered dreams,
In its strength, the world redeems.

Every heartbeat, a rhythm shared,
In the journey, we've all dared.
As bridges form from courage true,
Together, we'll build something new.

Towards tomorrow, we all stride,
With open hearts, arms open wide.
Through the years, we'll find our way,
On this bridge, forever we'll stay.

An Empty Stage Awaits

Curtains drawn, the spotlight glows,
An empty stage where silence flows.
Dreams are woven in the air,
Whispers of the show prepare.

The audience holds its breath tight,
Awaiting magic in the night.
From shadows, visions start to rise,
In every corner, a new surprise.

Moment's pause before the play,
Hearts racing, as we find our way.
Each role crafted from our core,
An empty stage has so much more.

With every act, emotions blend,
Stories told that never end.
As laughter, tears touch the soul,
In this space, we become whole.

The final bow awaits in time,
To honor stories and the rhyme.
An empty stage, our canvas bright,
Where dreams ignite in purest light.

The Magic of Tomorrow

In twilight's grasp, dreams unfold,
A tapestry of wonders told.
The magic glimmers like a spark,
Illuminating paths in the dark.

Tomorrow's whispers fill the air,
With hopes that dance and never scare.
Each moment brings a brand new song,
A melody where we all belong.

Curiosity fuels the chase,
In every heart, a secret place.
With every dawn, our spirits soar,
The magic of tomorrow, we adore.

Hands united, we chase the light,
In shared dreams, our futures bright.
Through every step, together we stride,
In the magic, we shall abide.

So let us weave a brighter fate,
With courage growing, never late.
For in the dawn, we're not alone,
The magic of tomorrow is our own.

Turning Leaves

Colors dance in autumn's breeze,
Whispers soft between the trees.
Golden crowns begin to fall,
Nature's beauty, wild and small.

Crisp air beckons, night's embrace,
Changing seasons, time won't pace.
Mirrored stillness in the brook,
Reflecting stories, nature's book.

Joyful flutters, wings take flight,
Morning's glow, a soft restart.
Fading warmth from summer's glow,
Echoes linger, then they go.

Fresh Tracks in the Snow

Blanket white upon the ground,
Quiet whispers, no sound found.
Footprints mark the path anew,
Nature's canvas, crisp and true.

Each crunch underfoot tells a tale,
Winter's magic, bright and pale.
Children laugh, snowflakes spin,
In these moments, joy begins.

Sleds glide down the hills so steep,
Cold winds chase, but hearts don't weep.
Cocoa warms from hands to soul,
In the winter, we feel whole.

Old Roots, New Soil

Deep beneath, where secrets lie,
Whispers echo, time goes by.
Ancient strength in every vein,
Memory woven through our pain.

Fresh soil welcomes life anew,
Sprouts of hope breaking through.
Each bloom tells of battles fought,
In every petal, lessons brought.

The past and present intertwine,
Nature's rhythm, pure design.
Together they create a song,
In unity, we all belong.

Unraveling the Past

Threads of time unravel slow,
Stories waiting, yet to show.
In the shadows, whispers dwell,
Echoing the truths we tell.

Memories hidden, dust-covered,
Layers peel back, hearts uncovered.
Each chapter filled with love and loss,
In tangled webs, we bear our cross.

Finding meaning in each twist,
In the dark, we can't resist.
Searching through the years gone by,
To embrace the reasons why.

A New Dawn Breaks

The sky ignites with hues of gold,
A gentle breeze begins to unfold.
Birds are singing, a sweet refrain,
As night retreats, it frees the pain.

Hope awakens with the light,
Chasing shadows, taking flight.
Every moment, fresh and bright,
Steps ahead in pure delight.

The world transforms, anew it glows,
Each heartbeat sparks, it softly grows.
Embracing change as fate bestows,
With open arms, the spirit knows.

In every dawn, a chance to rise,
To find the strength, to claim the skies.
A canvas wide, where dreams can soar,
A new beginning, forevermore.

Fresh Pages Unwritten

In the silence, thoughts take flight,
Blank pages wait, crisp and white.
Words unspoken, tales untold,
Mysteries wrapped in dreams of gold.

With every stroke, a story blooms,
Chasing away the lingering gloom.
Each letter dances, finds its place,
Creating worlds, breathing grace.

Past and future softly weave,
In every moment, we believe.
Here's where we find our inner voice,
In every word, a whispered choice.

Ink like rivers flows and streams,
Crafting life out of our dreams.
A journey starts with just one line,
Fresh pages echo, bright and fine.

The Rebirth of Dreams

Once they flickered, faint and shy,
Like distant stars in a clouded sky.
But hearts resurge with fiery will,
Awakening hope when dreams are still.

Buried deep but never lost,
Every heartbeat counts the cost.
From ashes rise, new visions gleam,
Reviving life, igniting streams.

Through trials faced and storms held tight,
Emerging stronger, ready to fight.
Let shadows fade, let courage beam,
In the dawn of the rebirth of dreams.

Infinite paths stretch ahead,
Each step taken, fear must shed.
For in rebirth, we learn to trust,
In dreams rejuvenated, bright and just.

Embracing Tomorrow's Light

As night surrenders to the day,
A brighter path comes into play.
With every breath, we witness change,
In the unknown, we find it strange.

But here we stand with hearts so bold,
Ready to write the stories told.
In the glow of morning's embrace,
We find our strength, we find our place.

Each ray of sun, a guiding hand,
Pointing us to a promised land.
With open minds and spirits bright,
We welcome all of tomorrow's light.

Let fears dissolve in warmth and grace,
For every moment, we must face.
Together we'll rise, take to the skies,
Embracing tomorrow, where hope lies.

Clearing the Fog

The morning mist begins to fade,
A world once lost, now displayed.
Soft hues emerge in gentle light,
Guiding all from dark to bright.

Steps once cautious, now feel bold,
Stories waiting to be told.
Each breath a spark, a chance to dream,
In the clarity, hope will gleam.

Branches stretch to greet the sun,
Nature stirs, a race begun.
With every whisper, life aligns,
In this moment, magic shines.

Past encounters fade away,
Future beckons, come what may.
Through the fog, we find our way,
In this new dawn, we shall stay.

Embrace the light with open hands,
Together strong, like ancient strands.
From shadowed paths to open skies,
The fog now clears, the spirit flies.

Sunlight on the Horizon

As dawn awakens the silent night,
A golden glow ignites our sight.
Promises linger in the air,
Hopeful hearts begin to share.

In the distance, rays unfold,
Stories waiting to be told.
Nature's canvas, painted bright,
Whispers of the morning light.

Clouds dissolve, the day starts anew,
Every heart beats, bold and true.
With every step, we break the chains,
Sunlight dances, joy remains.

The path ahead glimmers with grace,
In every shadow, we find our place.
Hand in hand, we stride as one,
Shining brightly 'neath the sun.

With each moment that we hold,
Adventures born, our spirits bold.
Together we rise, a timeless song,
Sunlight calls us to belong.

A New Chapter Unfolds

With every page, the story grows,
New chapters wait, the river flows.
In the silence, dreams take flight,
Eyes wide open, hearts igniting bright.

Yesterday's tales fade with time,
Each ending brings a chance to climb.
Winds of change sweep through our days,
Guiding us in wondrous ways.

Words unsaid now find their place,
Hopeful futures we shall embrace.
Navigating through trials ahead,
In this journey, we won't dread.

Empty spaces fill with dreams,
As life unfolds, or so it seems.
A blank canvas, colors bold,
With our stories yet untold.

Here we stand, ready to write,
Every heartbeat, pure delight.
As a new chapter begins to call,
Together we'll rise, together we'll fall.

Whispers of the Future

In the quiet depths of the night,
Dreams awaken, taking flight.
Softly they speak, a gentle sigh,
Lessons learned, as stars pass by.

Time unfolds, a dancing ghost,
Moments cherished, we love the most.
In the stillness, voices rise,
Whispers echo across the skies.

Paths unknown begin to form,
In this journey, we transform.
Guided by a light so pure,
Each heartbeat, an embrace, assured.

As we listen, let us believe,
In the magic that we weave.
Every hope, a seed we sow,
Whispers guide us, steady flow.

The future beckons, hands held tight,
In darkness found, we seek the light.
With every whisper leading the way,
Toward the dawn of a brighter day.

A Compass for New Beginnings

In the dawn of dreams anew,
Paths unfold like morning dew.
Each choice a step, a whispered light,
Guiding souls through day and night.

With courage found in every heart,
We tread the road to worlds apart.
The map we draw with hope and grace,
Leads us forth to our own place.

A compass set on stars so bright,
Navigating towards the light.
Hope's beacon shines, a steady flame,
In this journey, none the same.

With every twist, the future's near,
Embracing doubts, yet holding dear.
Together we will chart and steer,
Through new beginnings, cast off fear.

So let us rise, take hands and fly,
Under the vast and open sky.
In the realm of chance, we find,
A compass forged of heart and mind.

The Whisper of New Adventures

In rustling leaves, the secrets call,
Adventure waits beyond the wall.
A gentle breeze, a touch of fate,
Invites us forth, no time to hesitate.

With every heartbeat, a tale unfolds,
As laughter mingles with the bold.
Step lightly now, for dreams ignite,
In the shadows of the coming night.

The stars above, like gems alight,
Guide us onward through the night.
With open arms, we greet the dawn,
A symphony of life, reborn.

Through valleys deep and mountains high,
Together we will climb the sky.
Each moment shared, a treasure found,
In rivers wide and unmarked ground.

So heed the whispers, soft and sweet,
For adventure lies beneath our feet.
With every step, a story shares,
The world awaits, so take the dare.

Horizons Turned Gold

As twilight wraps the day in peace,
The horizon glows, our hearts in lease.
With radiant hues of orange and red,
New dreams arise, where old ones tread.

Each sunset whispers promises bright,
Of journeys waiting in the night.
With every glance, the world may change,
In every heartbeat, life's arranged.

Together, we will chase the glow,
Across the fields of all we know.
In the warmth of dusk, we find our way,
Threads of hope in the fading day.

Embrace the gold that marks the end,
For with each close, a chance to mend.
In gathering light, we rise anew,
Horizons turn as dreams come true.

So let us venture, hand in hand,
With hearts aligned and spirits fanned.
Through gilded skies and open doors,
Life's possibilities—forever ours.

Beyond the Veil of Yesterday

A shroud of dreams, the past remains,
Yet whispers urge us to break the chains.
Beyond the veil where memories lie,
The future beckons, bright and spry.

With every step, the shadows fade,
As hope awakens, unafraid.
Through tangled paths, we seek the sun,
In unity, we'll come undone.

Past echoes linger, soft and light,
Guiding us from dark to bright.
In every tear, a lesson learned,
In every smile, the heart has turned.

So let us sail on winds of change,
Embrace the new, let hearts arrange.
Beyond the veil, our spirits soar,
Into the unknown, forevermore.

With courage found, we journey forth,
To claim our dreams, our rightful worth.
For in the dawn of each new day,
Lies a path that leads away.

Uncharted Paths Ahead

In whispers soft, the journey calls,
With shadows long and evening falls.
New horizons, fresh and bright,
Step by step, we find the light.

Unseen roads stretch far and wide,
In every heart, a dream to guide.
Through tangled woods and winding streams,
We chase the echoes of our dreams.

The silent stars will light the way,
As night turns slowly into day.
With hopes unmasked and spirits free,
We write our tale of destiny.

The doubts may creep, the fears may rise,
But bold are those who dare the skies.
For in the midst of the unknown,
We find the strength to stand alone.

So here we stand, with hearts alight,
Embracing all with sheer delight.
In every step, a chance to be,
A voyage grand, our spirits flee.

When the World Awaits

A gentle breath upon the dawn,
With whispered dreams, we journey on.
The world unfolds, wide and vast,
Inviting us to sail at last.

With open arms, the future gleams,
Each moment built from hopes and dreams.
Together we will face the tide,
With courage fierce, we will not hide.

In crowded streets or quiet lanes,
We dance through joy, we wade through pains.
When shadows loom, hold fast your light,
For in the dark, we'll find our might.

Embrace the wind, the rain, the sun,
For every heart beats as one.
The world awaits; let's take the chance,
To weave our fate in life's grand dance.

With every step, we chart our path,
In laughter's echo, love's warm math.
The future calls, so bold, so bright,
Together we can touch the light.

Phoenix Rising from Ashes

From ember's glow, a spark ignites,
In darkest nights, we seek our rights.
The ashes fall, the past erased,
In flames of courage, we are embraced.

Rising high, the wings unfold,
A tale of strength, a heart of gold.
In colors bright, we take to flight,
Reborn from ruins, ready for light.

The echoes of the battles fought,
In every scar, a lesson taught.
With every tear that graced our face,
We find the power to embrace.

The fire within, a blazing torch,
Guides us forth on this bold porch.
Through trials faced and storms endured,
Resilience blooms, our spirits stirred.

So let us soar on winds of change,
In every heart, the hope is strange.
From ashes deep, we rise anew,
A phoenix born, courageous and true.

The Canvas of Second Chances

With every stroke, the colors blend,
A tapestry where hearts extend.
The canvas wide, awaits our hand,
To paint our dreams and understand.

In shades of sorrow, joy, and pain,
Each line a story, loss and gain.
We find the strength to start again,
The beauty found in life's refrain.

Mistakes may fall like autumn leaves,
Yet in their midst, new hope achieves.
A palette fresh, we dare to dream,
In every error, a chance to redeem.

With brushes poised, we make our mark,
In silent nights or days so stark.
With love and courage, let us enhance,
This canvas bright, our second chance.

Each hue a moment, vivid and bright,
Together we will spark the light.
In this vast world, we take a stance,
Creating art in life's grand dance.

The Promise of a Clear Horizon

In dawn's embrace, hope softly glows,
The horizon beckons, where the river flows.
Dreams woven in gold, on the canvas of sky,
Together we rise, as the world passes by.

Each step forward, a whisper of grace,
With every heartbeat, we find our place.
Through storms and shadows, we'll sail the seas,
In unity bound, a heart's gentle ease.

The mountains may rise, but our spirits soar,
With courage ignited, we dare to explore.
Beyond the horizon, our futures await,
A journey of faith, we craft our own fate.

Stars light the path, guiding us home,
In the dance of the night, we shall freely roam.
With dreams in our pockets, we'll claim our right,
To chase after dawn, to embrace the light.

So here's to the promise of what lies ahead,
In the arms of the world, where no need for dread.
Together we'll chase what the heart desires,
With hope in our souls, we'll stoke the fires.

An Invitation to Change

Under the moon, where shadows play,
A whisper of change calls night and day.
With open hands, let go of the past,
Embrace the new, make each moment last.

Leaves dance in the wind, a gentle sway,
Each breath we take shows the new way.
In the heart of the storm, we'll find our peace,
Transformation blooms, and worries cease.

The walls we built, now slowly fall,
In vulnerability, we find our call.
Embrace the unknown, feel the shift,
Life's precious gift is our greatest gift.

In every ending, a door swings wide,
With courage we step, let love be our guide.
The journey ahead, though fraught with strife,
Is painted with colors that pulse with life.

So heed the call, let your spirit rise,
Awake to the dawn, where the future lies.
In this radiant dance, freedom's decree,
Join in the rhythm, be wild, be free.

Harvesting Tomorrow's Light

Fields of dreams await the sun,
In the heart of the earth, our work begun.
With every seed, a promise unfolds,
A tapestry woven with stories untold.

Hands in the soil, we nurture and care,
For tomorrow's light, we willingly share.
With patience we tend, and hope takes flight,
Each tiny sprout brings the vision to sight.

Beneath the branches where shadows play,
The fruits of our labor guide the way.
In unity found, we gather the yield,
The bounty of love, in the harvest field.

As twilight descends, casting gold on the land,
Together we stand, side by side, hand in hand.
With grateful hearts, we welcome the night,
And dream of a future, all bathed in light.

So let us gather, with voices aligned,
For tomorrow's promise, let our hearts bind.
In the dance of the stars, our spirits take flight,
We're harvesting joy, in the glow of the night.

Step into the Unknown

A road less traveled lies up ahead,
Where fears take flight, and dreams are bred.
With every heartbeat, the courage will grow,
In the depths of the dark, we learn to glow.

With whispers of doubt urging you to stay,
Let hope be the compass, lead the way.
In the silence of night, find your own tune,
Dance to the rhythm, let your soul swoon.

With hesitant steps, but spirits aflame,
The world awaits, with no hint of shame.
The unknown may shimmer with shadows of fright,
But bravery blooms when we trust in the light.

Each moment a canvas, fresh and anew,
A palette of choices, skies wide and blue.
Release the anchor, set sail for the stars,
Explore the expanse that's truly ours.

So step into the unknown, embrace every chance,
With hearts wide open, we'll join the dance.
For in each path taken, with courage we find,
The beauty of living, heart, soul intertwined.

Breaking the Chains of Yesterday

In shadows deep, our past resides,
But hope, a flame, forever guides.
With every breath, we break away,
Embracing now, a brand new day.

The weight of sorrow starts to fade,
As strength within begins to invade.
We shatter walls, release the pain,
And dance beneath the falling rain.

Each memory, a lesson learned,
Through trials faced, our hearts have burned.
No longer bound, we rise and soar,
The chains of yesterday, no more.

With open arms, we greet the light,
As stars above begin to shine bright.
Together strong, we'll find our way,
In freedom's arms, we'll ever stay.

The journey's long, but hope prevails,
Through every storm, our spirit trails.
In unity, we claim our dreams,
Breaking the chains, or so it seems.

A Symphony of New Beginnings

The dawn arrives with gentle grace,
A canvas bright, a sacred space.
Each moment new, a song to sing,
Life's orchestra begins to ring.

With every note, our hearts take flight,
In harmony, we chase the light.
A symphony of hopes and fears,
Composing dreams throughout the years.

The melodies of laughter blend,
As friendships form and spirits mend.
Through every change, we rise and flow,
Embracing paths we do not know.

The rhythm beats within our souls,
In every quiet, fleeting role.
We find our place, we play our part,
Creating music from the heart.

So let us dance to life's sweet tune,
As stars align beneath the moon.
In this new world, we boldly sing,
A symphony of everything.

The Art of Letting Go

In silent whispers, truths unfold,
As time begins to wear the bold.
We learn to release, to set things free,
The art of letting go, you see.

The past, a ghost that lingers near,
Yet liberation brings us cheer.
With open hands, we drop the weight,
In freedom's breath, we find our fate.

Old wounds may ache but heal with grace,
As light breaks through, we find our place.
Acceptance blooms where pain once grew,
The art of letting go feels true.

We paint our lives with vibrant hues,
Fading the shadows, we choose our views.
In every loss, a chance to start,
Releasing burdens heals the heart.

So trust the journey, embrace the flow,
In every ending, new seeds we sow.
With gentle hands, let go the past,
The art of letting go, steadfast.

Blossoms from the Ruins

Amidst the ashes, beauty grows,
In silent strength, the spirit shows.
From fractured earth, new life shall spring,
Blossoms from the ruins take wing.

The scars of struggle tell a tale,
Of resilience found when others fail.
Through storms we've faced, we've learned to stand,
A garden blooms from grief's own hand.

With roots entwined, we find our peace,
In every challenge, love's increase.
The petals soft, they catch the sun,
In unity, we've just begun.

Through every rain, each drop a grace,
Reminds us of our rightful place.
Together strong, we rise and grow,
In life's embrace, we'll boldly flow.

So cherish life, its twists and turns,
In every loss, a heart that yearns.
From ruins deep, our spirits soar,
Blossoms from the ruins, evermore.

Threads of New Beginnings

In the morning light we find,
Dreams are woven, softly intertwined.
Each thread a hope, a story spun,
New chapters birth with the rising sun.

Whispers of the future call,
Colors bright, they'll never fall.
With courage strong, we'll step ahead,
Embracing paths where fears have fled.

In gardens lush, we plant our seeds,
With love and care, we'll meet the needs.
Each bloom a chance, a star shall rise,
Brightening the darkened skies.

As seasons change, we learn to grow,
From every high to every low.
Together we stand, hand in hand,
In this new world, so vast and grand.

So let us walk with hearts aglow,
Through every storm, through every flow.
On threads of new, we stitch our fate,
Awakening dreams, it's not too late.

Reawakening the Dreams

In quiet moments, shadows fade,
A spark ignites, hope's serenade.
Whispers of wishes rise once more,
Unlocking dreams long lost before.

With every breath, a chance to soar,
The heart's desire, an open door.
Reach for the stars, let worries cease,
Embrace the journey, find your peace.

Through tangled paths and winding ways,
We dance with light on hopeful days.
The past may linger, but we are free,
To chase the visions yet to be.

Listen closely to each beat,
The rhythm of dreams, a melody sweet.
In every heartbeat, life resounds,
Awakening dreams that know no bounds.

Together we rise, a symphony bright,
In shadows, we become the light.
Reawakening dreams that softly gleam,
We build the world from every dream.

A Whisper of Change

In the stillness, a voice so sweet,
A whisper carries on gentle feet.
Change is coming, like a breeze,
Bringing light amidst the trees.

From petal's fall to winter's edge,
Nature's promise, a sacred pledge.
With every breath, let go of fear,
A future bright, so crystal clear.

Embrace the dance, the ebb, the flow,
In every heart, where dreams can grow.
With courage sewn in every seam,
Weaving life into a vibrant dream.

The ground awakens, seeds ignite,
In vibrant colors, pure delight.
A whisper shared, a life rearranged,
In the stillness, we find the change.

Together we step, hand in hand,
Navigating this wondrous land.
A whisper of hope, a chance to be,
In every moment, wild and free.

Reimagined Horizons

Beyond the mountains, where dreams take flight,
We gaze upon vast horizons, bright.
With every dawn, new paths await,
In the tapestry of fate we create.

Stars above, a guiding light,
In darkest times, they shine so bright.
With open hearts, we dare to seek,
The language of love, both strong and meek.

Through valleys deep and rivers wide,
We journey on with hope as our guide.
Each step we take, new stories told,
In every heart, pure wonders unfold.

The horizon calls, that endless space,
Where dreams can roam, and hearts embrace.
Reimagine all that you can see,
In every moment, you can be free.

So let the winds of change now blow,
Through every doubt, through every woe.
Reimagined horizons, vast and grand,
Together we stand, hand in hand.

Beyond the Brokenness

In the shadows, light still gleams,
Whispers of hope in fragile dreams.
When hearts are cracked, they find their song,
A melody sweet, where we belong.

Through the pain, we learn to rise,
To find our strength in the goodbyes.
Broken pieces craft new art,
A tapestry woven from the heart.

In the silence, courage grows,
A river of healing softly flows.
Beyond the scars, a new path finds,
The beauty hidden in life's designs.

With every tear, a blossom blooms,
Out of the ashes, life resumes.
Embracing shadows, we take flight,
Beyond the brokenness, we find light.

Harvesting Tomorrow

Seeds of today, in soil they lay,
Beneath the sun's warm, gentle ray.
Each moment cherished, each dream sown,
A promise of future fully grown.

Clouds may gather, storms may roar,
Yet in the heart, we still explore.
Nurturing hope in every breath,
We dance with life, defying death.

With hands outstretched to the wide unknown,
We gather courage, we have grown.
Harvesting tomorrows in the now,
Believing in the "why" and "how."

In fields of dreams, where visions thrive,
We plant the seeds, we feel alive.
With every choice, a path we chart,
Harvesting joy, where love will start.

Unfurling Dreams

In the morning light, buds will bloom,
Unfurling dreams dispel the gloom.
Petals open to greet the day,
In fragrant whispers, hopes will play.

Every heartbeat, a story told,
Of quiet wishes and visions bold.
As laughter dances on the breeze,
We trace our dreams like swaying trees.

With each dawn, we shed the night,
Reaching upward, hearts take flight.
Unfurling dreams like sails unfurled,
We embrace the magic of this world.

In starlit skies, our dreams aligned,
Guided by love, we search and find.
With open hearts, we dare to believe,
In the power of dreams, we receive.

Breathing Life into Dreams

With every breath, we weave our fate,
Dreams take flight, we illuminate.
In the stillness, we hear the call,
To breathe in hope and rise from the fall.

Every vision, a radiant spark,
Lighting the path through shadows dark.
We gather strength from the silent night,
Breathing life into dreams, igniting light.

With open hands, we hold our wishes,
Crafting futures, fulfilling dishes.
As we dance on the edge of chance,
Breathing life into dreams—our dance.

In the vastness, possibilities shine,
Each heartbeat echoes the divine.
We breathe in courage, exhale our fears,
Breathing life into dreams throughout the years.

New Beginnings

The dawn breaks softly, a whispering light,
Casting shadows away, embracing the bright.
Each step we take, a story unfolds,
In the heart of the brave, a future that holds.

With every heartbeat, dreams take flight,
Moments of courage, banishing fright.
A path untraveled, a chance to renew,
In every ending, begins something new.

Leaves turn to gold, seasons must change,
In the dance of time, we find the strange.
Hope is the fragrance of blossoms in spring,
In every new start, a joy we can bring.

Waves of the ocean, they ebb and flow,
Life's gentle rhythms, a constant show.
Embrace the unknown, let go of the past,
With every new dawn, we rise up at last.

In twilight's grace, we find our way,
A tapestry woven, brightening the gray.
With hearts wide open, we welcome the day,
In new beginnings, we dare to stay.

A Fresh Canvas

Glimmers of color dance in the light,
A canvas awaits, pure and bright.
Brushes and dreams in eager hands,
Crafting our visions, as each stroke expands.

A splash of hope, a dash of cheer,
Every line whispers, drawing us near.
Layers of texture, stories untold,
In the art of creation, we watch it unfold.

The palette of life, rich and diverse,
Through each hue and shadow, we gently traverse.
Mistakes become beauty, an art form unique,
With each new attempt, the heart learns to speak.

In silence we ponder, in chaos we find,
The freedom to wander, so beautifully blind.
With every creation, a piece of the soul,
On a fresh canvas, we reach for the whole.

Framing our thoughts in vibrant display,
A masterpiece growing, come what may.
In colors of passion, we find our voice,
A fresh canvas beckons, inviting us to rejoice.

Phoenix Rising

From ashes we come, reborn anew,
With flames of the past, we break on through.
Wings of resilience, we stretch and soar,
In the heart of the fire, we learn to explore.

Each trial faced fuels the blaze,
In the glow of rebirth, we dance in a haze.
Emerging stronger, we claim our throne,
In the midst of the storm, we are not alone.

We carry the light, a beacon so bright,
Guided by dreams, we embrace the night.
The journey is timeless, the path is our own,
In every heart's ember, a spirit is grown.

The flames might flicker, but never they wane,
In the cycle of life, we learn through the pain.
With courage ignited, we rise from the fall,
Embracing our power, we answer the call.

A phoenix ascends, defying the gloom,
In the fire we find, life starts to bloom.
With each brave flight, our legacy sings,
Through ashes of doubt, we find our wings.

The Art of Reinvention

In the mirror of time, we see our face,
Shifting reflections, an endless grace.
With colors of change, we paint our fate,
Embracing the journey, we learn to create.

Layers of lessons, each one a thread,
In the fabric of life, we stitch what's been said.
Through valleys of doubt, we rise and we bend,
In the art of reinvention, we find a new friend.

The beauty of metamorphosis unfolds,
In whispers of courage, our spirit beholds.
A canvas of choices, we make and we break,
Every brushstroke a story, every choice we take.

From ashes to blossoms, the cycle must spin,
In the heart of the struggle, we find strength within.
With open arms, we greet what's to come,
In the art of reinvention, we constantly hum.

So dance through the change, let your heart lead,
In the garden of growth, find the seeds you need.
With every new dawn, there's a chance to begin,
In the art of living, we're free to reinvent.

Unwritten Pages

In the quiet of the night,
Dreams take flight, unseen,
Every breath a canvas white,
Stories waiting in between.

Ink does not yet touch the pen,
Whispers linger in the air,
What will be, what has been,
Each moment a hidden dare.

Pages flutter, hopes arise,
Sketches drawn with fleeting light,
Life unfolds in soft reprise,
A narrative not yet bright.

With each heartbeat, words ignite,
Promises of what could be,
In the shadows softly write,
Every thought a mystery.

Turn the corners, find the way,
Each new dawn, a fresh start,
In this book of endless play,
Unwritten pages hold the heart.

Resetting the Stars

Underneath the velvet sky,
Wishes weave like threads of gold,
Galaxies flicker, dreams don't die,
Timeless stories yet untold.

Planets spin in endless dance,
Cosmos stretching far and wide,
In the silence, find your chance,
Hearts align, the past aside.

Find the constellations bright,
Chart your course with patience true,
In the depths of endless night,
Every star reflects in you.

Hope ignites the darkest space,
Shadows fade with every spark,
In the universe we trace,
Guided by our inner mark.

With a breath, reset the stars,
Feel the magic in your bones,
No more fears about the scars,
Cosmic light will lead us home.

The Echo of Tomorrow

Footsteps fade along the street,
Memories whisper soft and low,
In the distance, time discreet,
Echoes of the life we know.

Future dances on the edge,
Promises in every sound,
Life unfolds, a sacred pledge,
Each heartbeat, a new profound.

Voices linger in the breeze,
Carrying hopes yet to rise,
In the rhythm, find your ease,
Daylight breaks with endless skies.

Dreams resound in every choice,
Every moment a refrain,
In the silence, hear your voice,
Life's tapestry in the grain.

Tomorrow whispers, don't despair,
Every echo leads the way,
With each thought, show you care,
The future dawns in bright array.

Second Chances

When the sun begins to rise,
Hope awakens with the light,
Every tear a sweet disguise,
Promises of futures bright.

In the shadows of the past,
Lessons learned, the pain we knew,
Now we stand, resolved at last,
Ready for what's fresh and new.

Open hearts can start again,
Every moment, a new choice,
Through the storms, through all the rain,
Find the strength inside your voice.

Forgive the fractures, heal the soul,
Every heartbeat brings new grace,
Life's a journey, seek the whole,
Embrace the change, find your place.

With each dawn, a gift to keep,
Second chances, bright and bold,
In the depth, our spirits leap,
A tale of love yet to be told.

A Breath of Possibility

In the stillness, dreams take flight,
Whispers of hope dance in the night.
Each heartbeat sings a brand-new tune,
Awakening stars beneath the moon.

A canvas blank, awaiting a mark,
Every shade holds a spark so dark.
In the silence, a voice appears,
Guiding us through laughter and tears.

With every step, the world unfolds,
Stories waiting to be told.
The future glimmers just ahead,
A path where all our fears are shed.

Embrace the chance, let courage soar,
Unlock the door to something more.
Breathe deep the air of what could be,
In every moment, choose to be free.

A breath of life, a chance to grow,
In every heart, a fire aglow.
Together, let's reach for the skies,
And light up the world with our cries.

Light Beyond the Tunnel

In shadows deep, we search for light,
A flicker found through endless night.
With every step, the darkness fades,
Hope ignites, a spark cascades.

A journey long, and yet we strive,
Gathering strength, we'll stay alive.
Each heartbeat echoes with our dreams,
Resilience flows like rushing streams.

A guiding star, so far yet near,
Its gleam ignites both hope and fear.
Through winding paths, we chase the sun,
Together, we are always one.

The tunnel's end, a golden glow,
A promise kept, a way to grow.
In unity, we break our chains,
And through the trials, love remains.

Step forth, brave souls, embrace the dawn,
For in the light, our fears are gone.
With open hearts, let courage swell,
A brighter future, ours to dwell.

Embracing Uncertainty

In chaos bright, we find our way,
A tapestry woven day by day.
With trembling hands, we carve our path,
In unknown realms, we find our math.

The winds may shift, but still we stand,
With open hearts, we take command.
Each choice a step, each step a dance,
In tangled webs, we find our chance.

A world unfurls with every turn,
In shadows cast, we cease to yearn.
The beauty lies in what's unknown,
In moments shared, we have grown.

Let fears dissolve like morning mist,
With every sigh, a chance to twist.
Embrace the waves, the ebbs they bring,
For in the storm, our spirits sing.

With open arms, we greet the night,
In uncertainty, we find our light.
Together, let's chase the vast unknown,
In these wild dreams, we are home.

The Dawn of a New Era

The sun ascends, a fresh embrace,
Awakening the dreams we chase.
With golden rays, the shadows part,
A brand-new chapter, a brand-new start.

In every heartbeat, fresh ideas rise,
Like daisies blooming beneath the skies.
With open minds, we seek to learn,
In every page, new pages turn.

Together, let's redefine the norm,
Embracing power in every form.
In unity, we'll plant the seed,
With love and courage, we shall lead.

Beyond the borders, dreams unite,
A tapestry woven, fierce and bright.
We'll bridge the gaps and mend the rift,
In every heart, a precious gift.

The dawn arrives, a promise clear,
In every echo, we persevere.
Together, we will rise and soar,
In this new era, forevermore.

When Shadows Fade Away

In twilight's gentle hold, we find,
The whispers of dreams, softly aligned.
Stars emerge from the veil of night,
Guiding our souls toward the light.

Each heartbeat echoes a tale untold,
As shadows retreat, and courage unfolds.
With every step, we chase the dawn,
In the embrace of hope, we are reborn.

The past may linger, but we move on,
Finding strength in bonds that have grown strong.
Together we stand, hand in hand,
In a world awake, forever planned.

The darkness whispers its final plea,
As we rise with grace, forever free.
In unity, we forge a new way,
When shadows fade, come what may.

So let us dance on this radiant stage,
Turning the page, we start a new age.
With hearts alight, we will explore,
A future bright, forevermore.

The Light After the Storm

When thunder roars and the skies weep,
Hope lies hidden in shadows deep.
But as the tempest bows and bends,
A brighter moment slowly ascends.

Raindrops glitter like diamonds rare,
Painting the world with sparkles of air.
The sun peeks through with a smile so warm,
Bidding farewell to the raging storm.

Flowers awaken, refreshed and new,
Their colors vibrant, kissed by dew.
In every petal, life's promise grows,
A reminder that healing always flows.

We gather strength from nature's grace,
As light replaces the storm's embrace.
With every dawn, we rise and strive,
Finding the courage to feel alive.

So hold on tight through darkest night,
For after the storm comes a day so bright.
With hearts aglow, we embrace the change,
In the light after storms, we'll rearrange.

A Pathway through Uncertainty

On winding roads where shadows blend,
Each choice we make, a journey's end.
Through misty paths and tangled trees,
We seek a whisper carried by the breeze.

With every step, the unknown unfolds,
Stories of bravery in moments bold.
Navigating doubts that cloud our way,
Yet in our hearts, a light will stay.

Questions linger like stars in the sky,
But trust the journey, let your spirit fly.
For every stumble, there's room to grow,
In the depths of chaos, faith will glow.

Companions found on this winding trail,
Together we rise, together we sail.
With hearts unbroken, we forge ahead,
In the arms of hope, our fears shed.

So when the path seems lost, unsure,
Remember the strength that might endure.
Embrace the journey, come what may,
For in uncertainty, we find our way.

Renewed Hearts in Motion

With every pulse, a chance to grow,
Renewed hearts beat, steady and slow.
In the dance of life, we find our place,
Moved by rhythm, governed by grace.

Through trials faced and lessons learned,
A fire within has brightly burned.
As seasons shift, we rise anew,
With spirits lifted, and skies so blue.

Together we weave a tapestry bright,
Of love and laughter, pure delight.
In every heartbeat, we feel the spark,
A symphony played in the depths of dark.

Let go of fears, embrace the chance,
In dreams awakened, our spirits dance.
For every ending is just a start,
In renewed hearts, we each play a part.

So as we journey, hand in hand,
United we stand, together we'll stand.
With every breath, we're bound to share,
A world transformed, if we just dare.

A Heart Resolves to Rise

Through shadows deep, a light will gleam,
A heart ignites, renewed with dream.
Every struggle, a step we climb,
In hope's embrace, we conquer time.

With whispered strength, we break the seal,
A bond unyielding, we shall heal.
Fears diminish, like mist in dawn,
A warrior's song, we march upon.

From ashes rise, like phoenix born,
Through trials faced, our spirits worn.
Yet in each crack, resilience glows,
A path unfolds, as courage grows.

We write our tale with each heartbeat,
In unity, we feel complete.
Together bound, we'll pave the way,
For brighter nights and bolder days.

For every tear, a strength revived,
In the depths of pain, we thrive.
A heart that dares to rise anew,
Will find its wings and break on through.

Seeds of Hope in Distant Soil

In barren lands, we plant our dreams,
With whispers soft, like flowing streams.
Each seed of hope, a promise made,
In hearts aglow, fears will fade.

Beneath the sun, or in the rain,
These tiny truths will break the chain.
Nurtured by love, through patient care,
A garden blooms, both bold and rare.

Roots intertwine, they're not alone,
Together strong, they've brightly grown.
Against all odds, they stretch and reach,
The lessons learned, the life they teach.

As seasons shift, and winds grow cold,
Our hearts will warm, with stories told.
From distant soil, we gather strength,
Bound by the journey, close in length.

So let us spread these seeds of light,
In every corner, day and night.
For from our hearts to earth's embrace,
Hope's radiant bloom is nature's grace.

Rediscovering Lost Horizons

In twilight's glow, we search our past,
For dreams once bright, now fading fast.
With tender gaze, we seek the dawn,
To find again what we have drawn.

The mountains called, but we lost track,
Through winding paths, we found our crack.
Yet still we yearn for what we knew,
The open skies, a world anew.

With every step, we chart the way,
Unraveling threads from yesterday.
In whispered winds, the answers lie,
Beneath the vast, embracing sky.

Through fields of gold, our spirits soar,
In every heart, a hopeful roar.
To hold the horizon, arms extend,
A journey cherished, never end.

So let us wander, hand in hand,
Rediscovering this sacred land.
For in each horizon, new and bright,
We find our joy and purest light.

The Wind of Change Whispers

A breeze stirs softly, carrying tale,
Of fleeting moments that softly sail.
Through branches swaying, secrets unwind,
The wind of change, a voice so kind.

It rustles leaves, a gentle plea,
To open hearts and set them free.
As seasons shift, we must adapt,
In every loss, new dreams are mapped.

From winter's chill to summer's glow,
In every heart, the embers flow.
A time to mourn, a time to rise,
With every tear, a new surprise.

In whispered words, we hear the call,
To stand as one, and never fall.
The winds embrace our hopes and fears,
In every gust, we dry our tears.

So let the wind sweep through our days,
With open arms, we'll find new ways.
For change will come with softest grace,
And in its arms, we'll find our place.

The Seeds of Tomorrow

In hands we hold the dreams we sow,
Each tiny seed a tale to grow.
With whispered hopes and skies of blue,
We plant our wishes, brave and true.

The earth awaits our gentle touch,
With patience deep, we crave so much.
For every sprout brings forth a chance,
To nurture life in nature's dance.

Through seasons change, our roots will find,
The strength to seek, the strength to bind.
In gardens bright, we'll watch them rise,
Beneath the sun, beneath the skies.

As blossoms open, hearts will swell,
With stories shared that time will tell.
For every flower that starts to bloom,
A promise shines, dispelling gloom.

So let us sow the seeds we dream,
With all our love, and all our gleam.
In every leaf, in every one,
We find our peace, we find our sun.

After the Storm

The clouds retreat, the sky breaks free,
A silver lining's victory.
Puddles gleam like diamonds bright,
Reflecting hope, a pure delight.

The air is fresh, the world anew,
Each drop reminds of skies so blue.
A gentle breeze begins to play,
Dancing leaves in soft ballet.

With every step on soaked terrain,
We find strength forged in the rain.
The earth now hums a vibrant tune,
As life returns beneath the moon.

From thorny paths, we rise again,
Through trials faced and dreams we gain.
The storm's embrace, a passage clear,
Leading us to what we hold dear.

So let us breathe in scents of earth,
And cherish all that comes to birth.
For after rain, there blooms the light,
A brighter day, a hopeful sight.

A Journey Reimagined

With every step, the path unfolds,
Past whispers lost and stories old.
We wander on through shadows cast,
In search of futures, free and vast.

Each twist and turn, a chance to find,
The essence of a vibrant mind.
Through valleys low and mountains high,
Our spirits soar, our hearts comply.

With open eyes, we seek the creek,
Where waters flow and dreamers speak.
A tapestry of colors bright,
In every shade, a spark of light.

Through trials fierce and moments sweet,
We'll gather courage, stand on feet.
In every heartbeat, every sigh,
We craft our tale, and reach for sky.

So let us walk these paths anew,
And guide each other on through blue.
A journey vast, forever grand,
Together side by side we stand.

Rediscovering Lost Light

In shadows deep, we often stray,
Yet hope awaits to lead the way.
With timid hands, we seek the spark,
To light the corners, banish dark.

With every tear, we shed the past,
A moment's pain, but joy comes fast.
For in our hearts, the fire glows,
A beacon bright that gently shows.

We gather strength from all that's real,
The bonds we form, the love we feel.
Each laugh we share, a star that gleams,
In darkest nights, it fuels our dreams.

Through whispered words and gentle hands,
We lift each other, make new plans.
For in the light we find our way,
To treasure all each dawning day.

So chase the shadows, hold them tight,
In every heart, rediscover light.
For from the depths, we rise again,
With hope reborn, where love begins.

A Journey Begins Anew

With dawn's light, hope unfolds,
Every whisper, a story told.
Paths unknown, yet hearts are brave,
In this moment, dreams we save.

Each step forward, a chance to grow,
Leaves of change begin to show.
New horizons, clear and bright,
We embrace the morning light.

Carried by winds of fresh intent,
To the horizon, we're firmly bent.
Waves of courage push us on,
Towards the place where fears are gone.

Amidst the valleys, where shadows play,
We find our strength along the way.
Hand in hand, we take the leap,
Into the future, wide and deep.

And as the sun begins to rise,
We chase our dreams across the skies.
A journey new, with spirits true,
Together starting life anew.

The First Step Forward

A trembling foot, the ground beneath,
The beat of hearts, the quiet breath.
In shadowed doubts, a spark ignites,
The first step taken, the world alights.

With every stride, a voice grows strong,
Melodies of courage, a vibrant song.
Paths once hidden now shine clear,
Guiding spirits, casting fear.

In the mirror, reflections show,
The faces of those who dared to grow.
With steady hands, we shape the day,
Carving dreams in bright array.

The road ahead may twist and bend,
But we walk forth, hand in hand, my friend.
With faith as our compass, we travel wide,
With every heartbeat, we turn the tide.

So let the journey draw us near,
As we face the dawn without the fear.
The first step forward, we take today,
A promise to never lose our way.

Echoes of Renewal

In silence deep, the echoes call,
Whispers of spring begin to enthrall.
Buds of green break through the frost,
Reviving dreams once thought lost.

Amidst the ruins, life persists,
In every shadow, a hopeful twist.
Nature's palette rich and bold,
Stories of rebirth waiting to be told.

Through the storms, we find our place,
Embracing time's relentless pace.
With each new dawn, a chance to rise,
Echoes of renewal fill the skies.

Hands raised high, we greet the sun,
With every heartbeat, work is done.
It's in the struggle, the pain we feel,
That the path to healing becomes real.

Collect the moments, let them weave,
A tapestry of what we believe.
In echoes sweet, the past will guide,
As we embrace the change inside.

Rewriting the Stars

In the cosmos, dreams collide,
With every wish, we play and glide.
Charting maps in skies so vast,
Rewriting futures from the past.

Galaxies spin with stories of old,
Secrets of heart in stardust told.
With courage, we defy the night,
Our spirits glowing, fierce and bright.

Through constellations, hopes are drawn,
Crafting a path until the dawn.
With every change, new worlds appear,
In the silence, the stars will hear.

Lines of fate, we twist and bend,
Dancing through time, hand in hand, my friend.
In each heartbeat, a wish ignites,
Rewriting the stars on shimmering nights.

So let us soar where dreams reside,
Where love and purpose coincide.
With every moment, we'll create the art,
Rewriting the stars, a map of the heart.

Breaking the Chains

In shadows deep, we hide away,
With weary hearts that beg to sway.
But strength within begins to rise,
To break the chains and claim the skies.

No longer bound by fear and doubt,
We stand tall, we scream, we shout.
The weight released, we feel the light,
In unity, we find our might.

Together forged, we find our way,
Empowered souls, come what may.
With every step, we burn the past,
In freedom's dance, we are steadfast.

The journey starts, the road unfolds,
In each new chapter, courage holds.
We'll weave a tale of strength and grace,
With love as our enduring base.

So break the chains and seek the dawn,
For in our hearts, true hope is drawn.
We rise anew, our spirits soar,
In every step, we're free once more.

Letting Go to Grow

In autumn's chill, leaves fall and fade,
A lesson learned, no need for trade.
To shed the past, we find our way,
Embracing change with each new day.

The weight of things we cannot keep,
We let them go, our souls to steep.
In empty spaces, seeds can grow,
From what we lose, our spirits glow.

Like winter's frost gives way to spring,
New life will burst when we take wing.
We trust the process, take our flight,
In letting go, we find our light.

The branches stretch, the flowers bloom,
From deeper roots, we conquer gloom.
In freedom found, we claim our voice,
In every end, we make a choice.

So let it go with gentle grace,
For every loss, a new embrace.
In letting go, we truly find,
The strength to bloom, the peace of mind.

The Path Less Traveled

A winding road, with twists and turns,
In every step, the heart still yearns.
With open eyes, we seek to see,
The truths that set the spirit free.

In brave pursuit, we face the night,
With dreams that guide us towards the light.
Each footfall whispers, 'Take a chance,'
In every moment, we find our dance.

Though fears may try to block our way,
We'll carve our path, come what may.
In solitude, we find our peace,
With every leap, our doubts release.

We gather strength from all we face,
In every trial, we weave our grace.
A tapestry of hopes and dreams,
On paths less walked, we forge our beams.

So journey forth, embrace the fright,
For in the dark, we find our light.
The path less traveled calls our name,
In courage bold, we stake our claim.

Blooming After Rain

When clouds above release their tears,
New life begins, as hope appears.
Through puddled streets and drenched terrain,
We rise anew, as blooms remain.

Each petal kissed by silver drops,
A vibrant dance where nature stops.
In every storm, a promise made,
We find our strength as colors fade.

The fragrant air, the vibrant hues,
In every heart, we find the muse.
Through cycles fraught with pain and plight,
We blossom forth, embracing light.

So let the rain wash woes away,
For in the dark, we find our sway.
With every storm that comes our way,
We learn to grow, we learn to play.

In blooming grace, we take our stand,
From weary roots, we stretch and span.
After the rain, we sing our tune,
With every dawn, we greet the bloom.

Like a Seed Beneath the Snow

In silence lies a hope so deep,
A promise held in winter's keep.
Beneath the frost, the soft earth sighs,
Awaits the warmth of springtime skies.

The layers thick, a secret bed,
Where dreams of green are softly bred.
Amidst the chill, a pulse remains,
A whispering life in frozen chains.

Time measured in the falling flakes,
Each one a note in nature's breaks.
They dance, they twirl, the cold winds blow,
Yet under wraps, the seeds shall grow.

With patience trusted, days draw near,
The sun will set the dormant clear.
From icy tombs, lush life will spring,
As warmth returns, the world will sing.

For like a seed beneath the snow,
Resilience thrives when winds do blow.
So hold on tight, though shadows cast,
The future bright, the storm shall pass.

The Call of Untamed Horizons

Beneath the vast and starry dome,
The winds of change beckon us home.
Each whisper carries tales untold,
Of distant lands and dreams of gold.

Beyond the hills, the rivers wind,
In every twist, new paths to find.
The call of nature pulls us near,
A symphony we long to hear.

With every step, the world expands,
The pulse of life in shifting sands.
In ancient woods, the echoes blend,
With lessons learned, our hearts transcend.

The sky ignites with hues so bright,
A canvas painted by the light.
Each horizon waits for those who roam,
To seek adventure, call it home.

A journey born of hope and stride,
Where wild and free, our dreams collide.
With every mile, our spirits soar,
The call of life forevermore.

Transforming Ashes into Dreams

In smoldering remains of what was lost,
Lies a beauty found, though pain the cost.
From ashes grey, the phoenix will rise,
A brand new dawn in the barren skies.

Each ember glows with stories old,
Of battles fought and hearts turned bold.
The fire ignites, a cleansing flame,
From darkened nights, we find our name.

In loss, we find a sacred space,
Where hope begins to trace its grace.
With courage drawn from shadows past,
New visions light the way at last.

From dust we came, to dust we go,
Yet in between, our spirits grow.
Transforming pain to vibrant schemes,
In every heart, a dream redeems.

So gather round the glowing coals,
In every heart, a spark consoles.
Through trials faced, we find our ways,
Transforming ashes into days.

A Voyage to the Unfamiliar

With sails unfurled, we set our course,
Upon the waves, we find our force.
The compass spins, unknown awaits,
Adventure calls, it never waits.

Each gust of wind, a song we chase,
In distant lands, we find our place.
The ocean's breath, a calming balm,
In every storm, we seek the calm.

As shores approach, new faces greet,
In foreign tongues, the hearts do meet.
With open minds, we bridge the gap,
In every hug, the world's a map.

From mountain peaks to valleys low,
The beauty of the unknown we sow.
Each step we take, new wonders grow,
A voyage bright, our spirits flow.

In every harbor, tales we weave,
Of friendships formed and nights to leave.
A journey vast, with memories dear,
A voyage to hold eternally near.

Rebirth in Bloom

In the garden, petals unfold,
Colors vibrant, stories untold.
Fresh dewdrops glisten in the light,
Nature awakens from the night.

Life returns with gentle grace,
Every bud finds its new space.
Birds sing sweetly in the air,
A symphony beyond compare.

Roots dig deep in the fertile ground,
In every corner, joy is found.
Hope arises with every bloom,
Filling every heart with room.

Sun shines bright, shadows dissolve,
In this dance, all hearts evolve.
Each moment, a tender embrace,
Rebirth sings in every place.

Celebrate this vibrant new,
Life awakens, fresh and true.
In every breath, a chance to thrive,
In this garden, we come alive.

Embracing the Dawn

A blush of light on the horizon,
Casting shadows of what's gone.
Morning whispers secrets bold,
A brand new canvas to unfold.

Golden rays kiss the dew,
Painting dreams with every hue.
Nature takes a breath so deep,
Awakening from restful sleep.

Birdsong flutters through the trees,
Carried on the gentle breeze.
Footsteps follow where light leads,
In each moment, hope proceeds.

With every step, we shed our fears,
Washing away the night's tears.
A promise held in the bright morn,
In every heart, a new day is born.

Embrace the dawn, let worries fade,
In the light, be unafraid.
With open arms, we greet the fire,
Igniting dreams, lifting desire.

From Ashes to Change

In the stillness, embers glow,
Beneath the ashes, life will grow.
Every end's a new beginning,
In this cycle, hope keeps spinning.

Through the fire, we find our way,
Lessons learned, we seize the day.
What was lost is now reborn,
In the light of a brighter dawn.

Silent whispers of the past,
Crafting futures, built to last.
Wounds may ache, but strength will rise,
From brokenness, we touch the skies.

Let the winds of change blow free,
Carrying seeds of bravery.
Every step, a chance to mend,
What was broken can transcend.

From ashes, we emerge anew,
With every breath, we start to view.
The beauty lies within the flame,
In transformation, we reclaim.

Journey of Renewal

On the path, the shadows play,
Guiding footsteps along the way.
With every step, a story grows,
In gentle whispers, wisdom flows.

Mountains tall and valleys low,
Every turn, a chance to grow.
In the struggle, strength is found,
Through the silence, life resounds.

A river flows, both wild and tame,
Carving valleys, calling names.
Through turbulence, we learn to bend,
Navigating paths around each bend.

Sunset fades, but stars ignite,
Guiding dreams into the night.
In every heart, a compass true,
Leading journeys, old and new.

With open skies, horizons wide,
Embrace the changes, let them guide.
The journey sings its timeless song,
In renewal, we all belong.

The Heart's Compass

In silence deep, the heart does know,
Its whispers guide where shadows flow.
Each beat a map, a truth to find,
In every pause, a spark aligned.

Through winding paths and storms that roar,
The compass points to love's great shore.
With every choice, the light expands,
Embracing all with open hands.

When doubt clouds skies and fears arise,
The heart's soft voice, it will advise.
A gentle nudge, a steady grace,
Leads us toward our rightful place.

As stars emerge in night's embrace,
The heart reveals its sacred space.
Trust in the journey, step by step,
For every move, a dream adept.

So heed the call, let courage swell,
For in this truth, all will be well.
With every beat, the path grows clear,
The heart's compass draws us near.

A New Horizon Beckons

From ashes rise a world anew,
Where hope ignites in morning dew.
The sun, it breaks, with golden light,
Inviting dreams to take their flight.

Across the fields where shadows played,
A vibrant heart, no longer swayed.
With every dawn, a choice appears,
To cast aside the weight of fears.

The winds of change, they softly call,
Through valleys low and mountains tall.
With every step, the future gleams,
A tapestry of woven dreams.

Embrace the chance, let passions flow,
For in this dance, our spirits grow.
A new horizon waits in view,
Awakening the brave and true.

So take a breath, release the past,
In every heartbeat, joy amassed.
With arms wide open, joy will find,
A new horizon, life unconfined.

Unearthed Potential

Beneath the surface, treasures lie,
In hidden depths, our spirits sigh.
The whispers of the past resound,
As dreams await to be unbound.

With every challenge, growth occurs,
The seedling wakes, the heart stirs.
Through trials faced and shadows cast,
The strength within will hold fast.

Awaken now, the time is near,
To shed the doubt, to face the fear.
In every tear, a lesson learned,
A fire ignites, a passion's burned.

With vision clear, we claim our space,
Unearthed potential, dreams we chase.
Together we rise, and never fall,
For deep inside, we hold it all.

So trust the journey, step by step,
Embrace your path, in faith adept.
The world awaits, your light will shine,
In every heartbeat, you're divine.

Painting with New Hues

With every stroke, emotions blend,
A canvas vast, where colors mend.
In shades of joy and hues of grace,
We find our truth, in this embrace.

The palette rich, our journey bold,
In every splash, a tale unfolds.
With whispers soft, the brush will dance,
Inviting hearts to take a chance.

From misty grays to vibrant reds,
Each color calls, the spirit spreads.
With mindful strokes, we shape our fate,
Creating worlds where dreams await.

As layers build, we come alive,
In every shade, our hopes derive.
From canvas white to vibrant view,
We paint our lives in colors new.

So take the brush, let passions flow,
With every hue, let visions grow.
In this great art, we find our way,
Painting with new hues, come what may.

Mosaic of Hope

In pieces we stand, so bright,
Each fragment a dream, a light.
Together we craft, hand in hand,
A vision of futures, so grand.

Colors collide, hearts entwined,
In the chaos, peace we find.
With every shard, a story to tell,
In this mosaic, we rise and dwell.

Hope is a thread, woven tight,
In the tapestry of the night.
From brokenness, beauty grows,
A dance of life, as hope bestows.

As dawn breaks through the shadows,
New journeys begin, hope flows.
With every step, we make our mark,
A canvas alive, igniting the spark.

So here we stand, hearts aglow,
In the mosaic where dreams sow.
A future bright, our mainstay,
In unity, we'll find our way.

Shattered but Whole

In silence, we gather the shards,
Each piece tells a tale, like cards.
With tender hands, we start to mend,
From brokenness, friendships blend.

Fractured whispers, secrets told,
A tapestry woven, brave and bold.
Though cracks remain in the design,
In every fracture, strength we find.

The wounds may ache, but we are strong,
In harmony's echo, we belong.
Through the pain, we rise anew,
Shattered spirits, yet shining through.

Like a phoenix, we take to flight,
With every struggle, we gain our might.
A puzzle complete, though pieces stray,
Together, we chase the night away.

In unity lies our greatest goal,
For we are shattered, but we are whole.
In this journey, hand in hand,
We'll face the world, strong we stand.

The Turning of the Tide

The waves crash in a rhythm clear,
Each ebb and flow, a tale to hear.
Change is coming, bold and fast,
The moment's here, we seize at last.

Seas may rise, and storms may roar,
Yet we are anchored, firm on shore.
With hopes afloat on waters wide,
We greet the dawn, the turning tide.

In stillness, whispers of the breeze,
A promise made, 'neath swaying trees.
Together we stand, hearts aligned,
Embracing change, new paths defined.

With every surge, our fears will fade,
As hand in hand, we're unafraid.
The tide will turn, a brand new day,
In unity, we'll find our way.

So let the currents pull us near,
In every wave, there's no more fear.
For with the tides, we rise and glide,
Together we'll journey, side by side.

Shadows Fade Away

As dusk falls softly, shadows creep,
In the silence, secrets keep.
Yet in the night's embrace we see,
That shadows fade, and we are free.

Stars ignite in the velvet sky,
Whispers of hope, a gentle sigh.
With every breath, the past will wane,
For in the dark, we shed our pain.

When morning breaks, we'll greet the sun,
Together, a new day has begun.
The shadows that once held us tight,
Now scatter swiftly in the light.

In every heart, a flicker grows,
As optimism in us flows.
For out of darkness, strength is born,
From shadows' grasp, we rise, reborn.

So let the light illuminate,
The path ahead, we will create.
For shadows fade, as dreams take flight,
In every heart, a spark ignites.

Roots in New Soil

Beneath the earth, the whispers sigh,
New roots stretch deep, they yearn to fly.
In unseen realms, they seek the sun,
From past to present, a journey begun.

Tangled with dreams, they intertwine,
Embracing change, they redefine.
Through storms that come, they hold their ground,
In enriched layers, hope is found.

In gentle rains, old fears dissolve,
With every sprout, their strength evolves.
Nature's gifts, a sacred trust,
In fertile soil, we turn to dust.

Together they thrive, in vast array,
With life anew, they pave the way.
Each leaf a promise, each bud a chance,
From roots in new soil, they dance.

Seasons change, yet still they grow,
In harmony, they learn to flow.
Boundless potential, they rise above,
Roots in new soil speak of love.

Embrace the Unfamiliar

Step into shadows, let courage ignite,
In realms unknown, hold your heart tight.
New faces, new places, a world to explore,
Open your spirit; there's so much in store.

Each turn brings lessons wrapped in surprise,
In every encounter, wisdom will rise.
The road may be rough, but the treasures are real,
Trust in the process; it's part of the deal.

Hearts intertwined, stories unfold,
Embrace the unfamiliar; be brave, be bold.
In the tapestry woven, threads brightly gleam,
Dare to dive deep into the dream.

Let curiosity guide where you roam,
In chaos find beauty, in strangeness, your home.
With every step, new visions align,
Embrace the unfamiliar; let your light shine.

With arms open wide to the vast unknown,
Find strength in the journey, in seeds that are sown.
A symphony played in each heart's refrain,
Embrace the unfamiliar; break every chain.

The Light at the Edge

At the twilight's realm where shadows meet,
A flicker shines, bold and sweet.
It beckons softly, a beacon so bright,
Guiding lost wanderers into the night.

In the hush of dusk, hope kindles anew,
Tales of resilience in every hue.
Though fears may ripple, faith holds tight,
The light at the edge promises flight.

Cradled in whispers, dreams take their form,
Hearts beat louder, defying the norm.
Fear fades to silence as courage unfolds,
The light at the edge is a treasure untold.

Together we rise, hand in hand,
With visions unbroken, dreams unplanned.
In every heartbeat, a story unwinds,
The light at the edge, where love always finds.

As dawn approaches, shadows retreat,
With every step forward, the journey's complete.
In luminous grace, our spirits converge,
The light at the edge as we merge.

Sculpting New Realities

With hands of intention, we shape the clay,
Molding our visions, come what may.
In the studio of dreams, where true hearts collide,
Sculpting new realities, let passion be your guide.

Gentle strokes of courage carve out the path,
Transforming the silence, releasing the wrath.
With each breath taken, the canvas expands,
Sculpting new realities with open hands.

Through layers of doubt, we press and we mold,
Unraveling stories that yearn to be told.
Each crack and each curve, a lesson embraced,
In the art of creation, find strength interlaced.

The future unfolds with visions in stride,
In the dance of the heart, let creativity guide.
Together we forge, amidst challenges faced,
Sculpting new realities, in hope's warm embrace.

As the masterpiece forms, a heartbeat defined,
In shared aspiration, true beauty aligned.
Through trials and triumphs, watch the dream soar,
Sculpting new realities, forever explore.

Recasting the Narrative

In shadows cast from what we've known,
We find the strength to stand alone.
The tales we tell can shape our fate,
With courage born, we won't wait.

New chapters call, with voices strong,
A future bright where we belong.
We write the words, we craft the theme,
In every heart, ignite a dream.

The past may haunt but we reclaim,
Our stories change, the rules, the game.
With every challenge faced anew,
We rise as one, a vibrant crew.

Beyond the pain, a lesson learned,
In unity our spirits burned.
Together we rewrite the lore,
Each sentence bold, we will explore.

So let us weave a brighter tale,
With threads of hope, we will not fail.
Recasting lives, a chance to thrive,
In every heart, our dreams will dive.

The Dawn of Renewal

A whisper stirs within the night,
As darkness fades, we seek the light.
The dawn unfolds, the shadows part,
New beginnings warm the heart.

With every ray, the world awakens,
Soft petals bloom, life unshaken.
In every breath, a chance to grow,
Embrace the change, let brilliance flow.

Hope arises with the sun,
In every dream, a new day begun.
Past sorrows fade, like morning mist,
In the warmth of light, we all exist.

The canvas waits for strokes so bold,
Each color bright, a story told.
Step with courage, let joy abide,
In the dawn, where love resides.

Together we shall dance and sing,
Embracing all the gifts life brings.
In harmony, our spirits soar,
The dawn of renewal, forevermore.

A Voyage into the Unknown

Beneath the stars, the ocean glows,
A ship sets sail where adventure flows.
With whispers strong and hearts so bold,
We journey forth, new tales unfold.

The winds of change ignite our dreams,
Through stormy seas and sunlit beams.
The horizon calls with its sweet song,
In every heartbeat, we belong.

Charting paths where no maps guide,
With every wave, we'll trust the tide.
Together facing fears unknown,
In unity, our courage grown.

The stars above, our navigators,
As we transform into creators.
A voyage grand, with hearts on fire,
In discovery, we find our desire.

So let us brave the endless night,
With dreams as sails, our spirits light.
Into the unknown, we set forth,
In this grand journey, find our worth.

Healing in the Unfolding

In quiet moments, peace descends,
With every breath, the heart mends.
The layers peel, the truth revealed,
In gentle waves, our wounds healed.

Through trials faced, we gather strength,
Each step forward, a tale of length.
With every tear, a river flows,
In vulnerability, the spirit grows.

The sun will rise, a beacon bright,
In darkness found, we seek the light.
With open hearts and healing hands,
We weave a tapestry that stands.

This journey's rich, with twists and turns,
In every challenge, the spirit learns.
Embracing all, the scars we bear,
In the unfolding, we find care.

So take a breath, let hope ignite,
In healing moments, claim your light.
Together as one, our stories blend,
In love's embrace, we finally mend.

In the Wake of the Past

Memories linger in fading light,
Echoes of laughter, shadows of fright.
Time whispers softly, a bittersweet song,
Carried on breezes where we still belong.

Faded pages, stories untold,
Lessons in sorrow, treasures of gold.
Each moment a thread in our woven tale,
With heartbeats that quicken, we will prevail.

Fields of old dreams and paths overgrown,
Searching for places we've seldom known.
In the silence, we hear the call,
In the wake of the past, we stand tall.

Starlit nights and the cloak of dawn,
A tapestry rich, where we have drawn.
We gather the pieces, stitch them with care,
In the wake of the past, our hearts laid bare.

From roots that have buried, we rise anew,
Embracing the moments and avenues.
With courage and love, we'll forge a new way,
In the wake of the past, we shape our day.

A Bridge to New Destinations

A bridge of dreams spans the open blue,
Inviting the hearts that yearn to pursue.
Footsteps of hope on this path we tread,
With visions of futures, where fears are shed.

Under the arch, the waters flow free,
Reflecting the light of what's meant to be.
With each gentle step, we reach for the sky,
A bridge to new destinations, we fly.

Beneath the vast heavens, skies softly call,
Whispers of promise in shadows that fall.
Together we'll venture, hand in hand side by side,
Across this great bridge, in unity, we stride.

The lanterns of dreams guide our way,
Illuminating paths where worries decay.
With laughter and love, we chase down the dawn,
A bridge to new destinations, we've drawn.

With every heartbeat, the future unfolds,
Pages unturned, with mysteries bold.
We journey together, our spirits align,
A bridge to new destinations, divine.

Wandering into Fresh Skies

Beneath the vast canvas of azure hue,
We wander softly, embracing the new.
A breeze on our faces, the sun's warm embrace,
Wandering into fresh skies, we find our place.

With every step taken, the world expands,
Nature's sweet whispers guide soft, gentle hands.
Mountains and valleys unfold on our quest,
Wandering into fresh skies, we feel blessed.

The scent of the wild, a floral delight,
Awakening dreams in the hush of the night.
We dance with the stars and leap with the tide,
Wandering into fresh skies, with hearts open wide.

Clouds, like promises, drift lazily by,
Painting our hopes in the boundless sky.
With laughter and light, we chase down the sun,
Wandering into fresh skies, we have begun.

In the journey of living, the path is our guide,
Wandering through moments, with love as our stride.
Together we travel, no destination set,
Wandering into fresh skies, we won't forget.

The Palette of Possibilities

Colors explode on the canvas of dreams,
Each stroke a promise, vibrant it seems.
With love as the brush, and hope as the hue,
The palette of possibilities, fresh and true.

Shadows and light dance in harmony's flow,
Creating a masterpiece that continues to grow.
In each quiet corner, a vision we find,
The palette of possibilities, intertwined.

From the depths of our hearts, new visions will rise,
Painting the world with laughter and sighs.
With whispers of courage, we embark on our quest,
The palette of possibilities, we manifest.

Imagination's spark ignites the divine,
Crafting our journeys through colors that shine.
With every bold stroke, we create our own fate,
The palette of possibilities, never too late.

So let's paint the canvas, each day a fresh start,
With dreams in our hands and love in our heart.
Together we'll flourish, let our spirits decree,
The palette of possibilities, just you and me.

A Future Untold Awaits

In shadows deep, dreams softly call,
Paths untraveled, we will not fall.
With hope as our guide, we'll reach for the light,
The stars will align, revealing our flight.

Together we'll weave the fabric of fate,
With courage, we step, before it's too late.
The whispers of time echo in our hearts,
As we journey ahead, each moment imparts.

A tapestry bright, of colors unknown,
In unity forged, our seeds will be sown.
With each rising sun, there's promise anew,
A future awaits, vibrant and true.

In laughter and tears, through all that we face,
We gather our strength in this sacred space.
With love as our compass, we'll write the next page,
For a future untold awaits on this stage.

So let us embrace what tomorrow may bring,
With open hearts ready, to dance and to sing.
For the journey is long, but together we'll stand,
Holding fast to the dreams that we cradle in hand.

Unfolding the Flower of Now

Petals unfurl in the morning's embrace,
Time blossoms gently, a tender grace.
In moments we savor, the beauty unfolds,
Each breath a reminder, as life gently molds.

A dew drop sparkling on leaves kissed by sun,
Whispers of wisdom, our spirits outrun.
Here in the present, we find our true worth,
Unfolding the flower, a miracle's birth.

The dance of the breeze through branches so high,
Invites us to linger, to dream and to fly.
In silence we listen, the world speaks aloud,
In the chaos of life, we are still and proud.

Every heartbeat echoes the song of today,
Guiding our steps, showing us the way.
With gratitude woven in each passing hour,
We blossom together, each moment our flower.

Let go of the past, the future can wait,
Each moment we cherish, we cultivate fate.
We are the essence, the bloom and the glow,
Living to marvel, unfolding the now.

The Gateway to Tomorrow

Beyond the horizon where shadows retreat,
Lies a gateway to dreams, where futures meet.
With hands outstretched, we shall venture forth,
Through realms uncharted, embracing our worth.

In the whispers of night, the stars call our name,
Igniting a fire, a passionate flame.
The doors of the future swing wide with a creak,
As we step through the veils of the dreams that we seek.

Each choice a ripple, each moment a thread,
We weave our own story, the life we have led.
In courage, we'll travel, fueled by our hearts,
Exploring the wonder, where adventure starts.

With every dawn breaking, our spirits take flight,
Into the unknown, the vastness of night.
No fear will deter us, with faith in our sight,
Together we'll dance in the dawn's early light.

So let us embark on this journey profound,
With dreams in our pockets, together we're bound.
The gateway to tomorrow will open its door,
As we step into magic, forever explore.

Ripples of Reinvigoration

In still waters deep, where silence resides,
Ripples awaken, as each moment glides.
With echoes of laughter, the heart finds its way,
Reinvigoration blooms, brightening the day.

From whispers of nature, we gather our breath,
As life spins anew, transcending all death.
In cycles of change, we rise and we bend,
Embracing the journey, as moments transcend.

With eyes wide open, we witness the flow,
Each ripple a message, each wave a new glow.
In unity's grace, we rise and we shine,
Reinvigoration calls, and our souls intertwine.

The pulse of the earth beats in sync with our own,
In harmony woven, we'll never be alone.
For together we stand on this canvas of grace,
With ripples of love making sacred our space.

So let us celebrate every wave that we face,
With courage and spirit, moving in place.
In ripples of reinvigoration, we soar,
Together we flourish, forever explore.

Reclaiming Lost Dreams

In shadows where hopes once lay,
Whispers of time drift away.
With courage we dare to rise,
To grasp the stars in far-off skies.

The echoes of laughter return,
As embers of passion now burn.
Through trials and heartaches we wade,
In starlight, our fears shall fade.

Each heartbeat a call to create,
A canvas where dreams resonate.
With every breath, we ignite,
Reclaiming our futures, so bright.

Together we'll weave our own fate,
With threads of love, never late.
In moments reclaimed, we'll find
The strength to leave doubt behind.

So here we stand, hand in hand,
With visions of joy, bold and grand.
With faith in our hearts that gleams,
We set forth to reclaim lost dreams.

Footprints in Fresh Snow

Upon the white, pure and deep,
Silent secrets, dreams we keep.
Each step a print, a tale to tell,
In winter's embrace, all is well.

Beneath the sky's soft silver glow,
We wander where the cold winds blow.
Every track speaks of our way,
As time melts into a new day.

With every footstep, we create,
A path to share, a choice of fate.
In crisp air, our laughter rings,
Listening closely, the joy it brings.

The world around, so still, so bright,
Holds promises wrapped in pure white.
Together, we freeze these moments here,
Footprints whispering love sincere.

As evening drapes the world in blue,
We find the warmth in each venture new.
For in this snow, our hearts align,
Footprints in fresh wonders, divine.

The Sound of New Beginnings

In the hush of dawn's first light,
A melody stirs, pure and bright.
With every note, we start anew,
A symphony of dreams in view.

Whispers of hope in the breeze,
Unfold in ways that aim to please.
An echo of laughter fills the air,
As time opens doors everywhere.

A gentle rhythm guides our feet,
As past and future joyously meet.
With every heartbeat, we embrace,
The sound of life, a warm embrace.

In moments stitched with vibrant thread,
The echoes of love dance ahead.
With each sunrise, we'll break the mold,
In unity, our stories unfold.

So let the music inspire and soar,
As we journey through this open door.
For in each note, our spirits sing,
In the sound of new beginnings, we bring.

Colors of a New Day

As dawn awakens with a smile,
The world dons colors, bright and mild.
Painting the sky with hues divine,
A canvas of dreams, yours and mine.

Glistening greens and vibrant gold,
Stories of life waiting to unfold.
Each shade whispers a tale of hope,
In beauty, together we cope.

Beneath the sun's warm embrace,
We find our rhythm, our space.
In every shade, a lesson learned,
The fire of passion forever burned.

As colors blend in sweet array,
We touch the dawn of a brand new day.
In every heartbeat, every ray,
We celebrate the colors at play.

So let us cherish this vibrant light,
As hearts converge, ready to ignite.
For in this palette, life's ballet,
We find our joy in a new day.